T0322874

W. S. GRAHAM

New Selected Poems

edited by Matthew Francis

FABER & FABER

First published in 2018
by Faber and Faber Limited
The Bindery, 51 Hatton Garden
London EC1N 8HN

Typeset by Reality Premedia Services Pvt. Ltd.
Printed in England by T J Books Limited, Padstow, Cornwall

A CIP record for this book
is available from the British Library

ISBN 978-0-571-34844-2

4 6 8 10 9 7 5 3

Contents

Introduction   vii

Over the Apparatus of the Spring is Drawn   3
O Gentle Queen of the Afternoon   4
Here next the Chair I was when Winter Went   5
My Glass Word Tells of Itself   6
Since All My Steps Taken   7
Listen. Put on Morning   8
Shian Bay   10
Gigha   11
The Nightfishing   12
from Seven Letters   30
from Two Ballads   34
The Dark Intention   39
Malcolm Mooney's Land   40
The Beast in the Space   45
The Constructed Space   46
The Thermal Stair   47
I Leave This at Your Ear   50
The Dark Dialogues   51
Approaches to How They Behave   59
Clusters Travelling Out   65
The Greenock Dialogues   70
What is the Language Using Us for?   76
Imagine a Forest   82
Enter a Cloud   84
Greenock at Night I Find You   88
Loch Thom   89
To Alexander Graham   91
Johann Joachim Quantz's Five Lessons   93
Lines on Roger Hilton's Watch   97
Implements in Their Places   99

Dear Bryan Wynter   117
To My Wife at Midnight   120
A Walk to the Gulvas   124
An Entertainment for W. S. Graham for Him
    Having Reached Sixty-five   126

Introduction

W. S. Graham's 'The Dark Dialogues' gives an atmospheric depiction of the Clydeside setting of his working-class childhood in the 1920s. In this dreamlike poem, with its shifting personae and voices, a stranger visits the 'land' or tenement building, number 1, Hope Street, where the young Graham lived with his family:

> Almost I, yes, I hear
> Huge in the small hours
> A man's step on the stair
> Climbing the pipeclayed flights
> And then stop still
> Under the stairhead gas
> At the lonely tenement top.
> The broken mantle roars
> Or dims to a green murmur.
> One door faces another.

The visitor may be a stand-in for the reader of the poem, or Graham himself, returning in ghostly form to visit his old home after years away; whoever he is, he is transformed a moment later into another 'stranger', a dialect word meaning a fluttering piece of ash in the fire, 'hissing in the grate'. Here we see some of the key themes of Graham's work: a deep love and nostalgia for his Scottish roots, an uncanny sense of his estrangement from them, and a keen understanding of the power of language both to evoke such experiences and to change them into something more abstract yet equally significant. Language can do amazing things in the right hands, as Graham notes when he uses it, in effect, to turn himself into his father:

> . . . through
> Nothing more than where

I am made by this word
And this word to occur.

It is understandable that, following his exposure to poetry and phi-
losophy at a Workers' Educational Association course he attended as
a teenager, he deviated from his projected career in the shipyards of
Greenock and chose to become a poet. Nevertheless, it was a decision
that was to involve much hardship. Following brief early spells in paid
employment, he lived a bohemian life in Cornwall with his wife Nessie
from the mid-1950s until his death in 1986, relying on the support of
friends who believed in his talent. Far more than the meagre diet and
the cottage lit by oil-lamps, however, it seems to have been the sense
of separation from his family and working-class community that dis-
tressed him, while at the same time providing both an incentive and
some of the material for his creative achievements.

The western tip of Cornwall was an exciting place for a man of
artistic interests in the 1950s. A new generation of abstract painters
had established themselves there, two of whom, Bryan Wynter and
Roger Hilton, became Graham's close friends and drinking compan-
ions, stimulating him to think deeply about the differences between
word and image as modes of artistic expression. He wrote moving
elegies for both friends, but his greatest exploration of this theme is
'The Thermal Stair', written after the death of another St Ives painter,
Peter Lanyon, following a gliding accident:

> The poet or painter steers his life to maim
>
> Himself somehow for the job. His job is Love
> Imagined into words or paint to make
> An object that will stand and will not move.

Cornwall, like the Firth of Clyde, was also a centre of the fishing
industry, and Graham drew on his own experiences of going out on
fishing boats for what is arguably his most ambitious poem. 'The
Nightfishing', first published in 1951, relates with extraordinary

vividness and precision of detail an expedition to catch herring. While the communal labour of the fishermen is going on, a solitary man is engaged in labour of a different kind, writing a poem, and the two events are mapped onto each other in a complex extended allegory: the poet trawls the dark sea of language to bring home a poem, just as the fishermen trawl the midnight Atlantic:

> Across our moving local of light the gulls
> Go in a wailing slant. I watch, merged
> In this and in a like event, as the boat
> Takes the mild swell, and each event speaks through.
> They speak me thoroughly to my faintest breath.
> And for what sake? Each word is but a longing
> Set out to break from a difficult home.

'The Nightfishing' impressed T. S. Eliot, who had taken on Graham's previous collection, *The White Threshold*, for Faber and Faber in 1949. At the same time, however, Eliot warned that 'it was "intellectual" poetry, and would go slow because people just were lazy about thinking'. On the whole, he was right: despite Eliot's support, Graham did not experience the spectacular rise to fame that such poets as Dylan Thomas, John Betjeman and his own close contemporary Philip Larkin enjoyed in the mid-twentieth century, and many of his admirers would argue that he has still not received all the acclaim his brilliance deserves. The reasons for this are complex, but one factor, undoubtedly, was the original forging of his career during the 1940s, when a dense and verbose style often referred to as 'neo-romantic' was all the rage. Graham participated in this trend, owing much to the influence of the neo-romantics' idol, Thomas, whose reputation was to plummet a few years later. Many poets who began at the same time, Larkin among them, were embarrassed by their early poems. Graham, on the other hand, stubbornly defended the difficult, exuberant contents of his first four collections, published in rapid succession between 1942 and 1949, for the rest of his life. By 1955, when *The Nightfishing* appeared, however, those days were behind him; the poems of this collection were rich and strange, but they were also mature and fully achieved, and, in hindsight, it seems an injustice that they were not more widely noticed.

Soon afterwards, though, his style began to change more radically. 'The Constructed Space' (first published in 1958) and 'The Dark Dialogues' (1959) were plainer in diction and more explicit in their self-reflexive treatment of his lifelong themes of language and poetic artifice. The Graham of the late poems, playful, paradoxical and disarmingly colloquial, was beginning to emerge, though it was not till 1970 that he published the first of his two great final volumes, *Malcolm Mooney's Land*. The fifteen-year gap that separates this from *The Nightfishing*, during which his profile in the poetry world was so low that his publishers are said to have thought he had died, has sometimes been seen as evidence of a conspiracy against him, the attempt by an anti-modernist poetic establishment to suppress a poet they saw as dangerously experimental. But Graham does not seem to have been making great efforts over this period to maintain his reputation (or, indeed, to remind his publisher of his continuing existence), and a more likely explanation is that such a profound change simply took a long time to complete.

The title poem of *Malcolm Mooney's Land* both set the tone (tragicomic) and established some of the key imagery (ice and snow) for his late poems. Mooney is a portrait of the poet as doomed Arctic explorer. The fact that his name was borrowed from a chain of pubs owned by the Guinness company – the twentieth-century equivalent of calling him Wetherspoon – suggests that we are to see him as an alter ego of his hard-drinking creator. He does his exploring in the wilderness of language, leaving his dark footprints on the whiteness of the page. We see Mooney writing his diary, irritated by the biting of insects that turn out to be words ('brother / To the grammar-sow and the wordlouse'), haunted by memories of human contact, with his wife and son and with other explorers. At one point he even thinks he hears a telephone ringing, the personal response to his utterances which no poet should expect. 'I am always very aware', Graham wrote later, 'that my poem is not a telephone call. The poet only speaks one way. He hears nothing back.'

It would have amused and gratified him, no doubt, to hear the increasingly loud chatter of readers responding to his work over the last few years. Since his death in 1986, the steady rise of Graham's reputation has been marked by regular publications, both critical works and new editions of his poetry. In 2004 I edited the *New Collected Poems* for Faber and Faber, restoring the early poems that had been omitted from the original *Collected Poems* of 1979 and adding a number of uncanonical pieces, including the contents of a pamphlet of *Uncollected Poems* (1990) and the manuscript poems first published as *Aimed at Nobody* (1993). Now, as we mark the centenary of his birth, celebratory events and readings are being held across the country, including a digital poetry residency called The Blue Crevasse at the Scottish Poetry Library. (One can only imagine how much he would have enjoyed the abstract space of the Internet.) A new anthology, *The Caught Habits of Language*, edited by Rachael Boast, Andy Ching and Nathan Hamilton, brings together poems in his honour by contemporary poets of many schools and styles, some older tributes by his contemporaries and some previously unknown poems by Graham himself. There could not be a more appropriate time for his publishers, Faber and Faber, to release this *New Selected Poems*, designed to introduce yet more readers to his oeuvre. I have chosen poems from every stage of his career, and attempted to represent the full range of his output, including uncollected material, arranging them roughly chronologically but retaining the order of the contents of his collections. I would like to thank the editors of *The Caught Habits of Language* for sharing one of the new discoveries, 'An Entertainment for W. S. Graham for Him Having Reached Sixty-five', which I have included as the final poem here. Special thanks to W. S. Graham's daughter, Rosalind Mudaliar, for her permission to publish the poems, and thanks also to Matthew Hollis, Lavinia Singer and Faber and Faber for their continuing support of this vitally important modern poet.

MATTHEW FRANCIS

NEW SELECTED POEMS

OVER THE APPARATUS OF
THE SPRING IS DRAWN

Over the apparatus of the Spring is drawn
A constructed festival of pulleys from sky.
A dormouse swindled from numbers into wisdom
Trades truth with bluebells. The result unknown
Fades in the sandy beetle-song that martyrs hear
Who longingly for violetcells prospect the meads.

As luck would testify, the trend for logic's sake
Takes place on pleasant landscapes within graves
That flesh, the sun's minister, in jealous agonies
Seeks out in choral vagaries with bird and blood.
Those funnels of fever (but melody to gales)
Tenant the spiral answer of a scarecrow daisy.

The country crimes are doctrines on the grass
Preaching a book of veins. The answer is order.
A derrick in flower swings evening values in
And wildernight or garden day frames government
For thieves in a prison of guilt. Birches erect
The ephemeral mechanism of welcoming.
And Spring conquests the law in a cuckoo's school.

O GENTLE QUEEN OF THE AFTERNOON

O gentle queen of the afternoon
Wave the last orient of tears.
No daylight comet ever breaks
On so sweet an archipelago
As love on love.

The fundamental negress built
In a cloudy descant of the stars
Surveys no sorrow, invents no limits
Till laughter the watcher of accident
Sways off to God.

O gentle queen of the afternoon
The dawn is rescued dead and risen.
Promise, O bush of blushing joy,
No daylight comet ever breaks
On so sweet an archipelago
As love on love.

HERE NEXT THE CHAIR I WAS
WHEN WINTER WENT

Here next the chair I was when winter went
Down looking for distant bothies of love
And met birch-bright and by the blows of March
The farm bolder under and the din of burning.

I was what the whinfire works on towns
An orator from hill to kitchen dances.
In booths below bridges that spanned the crowds
Tinkers tricked glasses on lips and saw my eyes.

Like making a hut of fingers cupped for tears
Love burned my bush that was my burning mother.
The hoodiecrow in smoke in a wobbling wind
If a look is told for fortune saw my death.

So still going out in the morning of ash and air
My shovel swings. My tongue is a sick device.
Fear evening my boot says. The chair sees iceward
In the bitter hour so visible to death.

MY GLASS WORD TELLS OF ITSELF

Writing this so quietly writes of itself.
So serving only cities falling in words
Round the dead guessed at fifty
In the petrol passover and the dribbling ink
Down hills of quick rubble,
I watch through a medal the drowning Noah sink.

Flood's animal calls each lifesize hill
A shoal, and the panorama of news
Floats man on cork.
Poor like a scribble my crime on a diamond
Is a gannet I am made in,
Not by your head but the beak of my diving hand.

Writing this so quietly writes of itself.
So saving only the seaport in a bottle
With a history of threads
On a told ship under the sky's green grave
On the sea's coloured oval,
I pour round glass the sand my rivers have.

SINCE ALL MY STEPS TAKEN

Since all my steps taken
Are audience of my last
With hobnail on Ben Narnain
Or mind on the word's crest
I'll walk the kyleside shingle
With scarcely a hark back
To the step dying from my heel
Or the creak of the rucksack.
All journey, since the first
Step from my father and mother
Towards the word's crest
Or walking towards that other,
The new step arrives out
Of all my steps taken
And out of today's light.
Day long I've listened for,
Like the cry of a rare bird
Blown into life in the ear,
The speech to that dead horde
Since all my steps taken
Are audience of my last
With hobnail on Ben Narnain
Or mind on the word's crest.

Listen. Put on morning.
Waken into falling light.
A man's imagining
Suddenly may inherit
The handclapping centuries
Of his one minute on earth.
And hear the virgin juries
Talk with his own breath
To the corner boys of his street.
And hear the Black Maria
Searching the town at night.
And hear the playropes caa
The sister Mary in.
And hear Willie and Davie
Among bracken of Narnain
Sing in a mist heavy
With myrtle and listeners.
And hear the higher town
Weep a petition of fears
At the poorhouse close upon
The public heartbeat.
And hear the children tig
And run with my own feet
Into the netting drag
Of a suiciding principle.
Listen. Put on lightbreak.
Waken into miracle.
The audience lies awake
Under the tenements
Under the sugar docks
Under the printed moments.
The centuries turn their locks

And open under the hill
Their inherited books and doors
All gathered to distil
Like happy berry pickers
One voice to talk to us.
Yes listen. It carries away
The second and the years
Till the heart's in a jacket of snow
And the head's in a helmet white
And the song sleeps to be wakened
By the morning ear bright.
Listen. Put on morning.
Waken into falling light.

SHIAN BAY

Gulls set the long shore printed
With arrow steps over this morning's
Sands clean of a man's footprint
And set up question and reply
Over the serpentine jetty
And over the early coaches
Of foam noisily in rows
Driven in from the farout banks.

Last gale washed five into the bay's stretched arms,
Four drowned men and a boy drowned into shelter.
The stones roll out to shelter in the sea.

GIGHA

That firewood pale with salt and burning green
Outfloats its men who waved with a sound of drowning
Their saltcut hands over mazes of this rough bay.

Quietly this morning beside the subsided herds
Of water I walk. The children wade the shallows.
The sun with long legs wades into the sea.

THE NIGHTFISHING

1

Very gently struck
The quay night bell.

Now within the dead
Of night and the dead
Of my life I hear
My name called from far out.
I'm come to this place
(Come to this place)
Which I'll not pass
Though one shall pass
Wearing seemingly
This look I move as.
This staring second
Breaks my home away
Through always every
Night through every whisper
From the first that once
Named me to the bone.
Yet this place finds me
And forms itself again.
This present place found me.
Owls from on the land.
Gulls cry from the water.
And that wind honing
The roof-ridge is out of
Nine hours west on the main
Ground with likely a full
Gale unwinding it.

Gently the quay bell
Strikes the held air.

Strikes the held air like
Opening a door
So that all the dead
Brought to harmony
Speak out on silence.

I bent to the lamp. I cupped
My hand to the glass chimney.
Yet it was a stranger's breath
From out of my mouth that
Shed the light. I turned out
Into the salt dark
And turned my collar up.

And now again almost
Blindfold with the bright
Hemisphere unprised
Ancient overhead,
I am befriended by
This sea which utters me.

The hull slewed out through
The lucky turn and trembled
Under way then. The twin
Screws spun sweetly alive
Spinning position away.

Far out faintly calls
The continual sea.

Now within the dead
Of night and the dead

Of all my life I go.
I'm one ahead of them
Turned in below.
I'm borne, in their eyes,
Through the staring world.

The present opens its arms.

2

To work at waking. Yet who wakes?
Dream gives awake its look. My death
Already has me clad anew.
We'll move off in this changing grace.
The moon keels and the harbour oil
Looks at the sky through seven colours.

When I fell down into this place
My father drew his whole day's pay,
My mother lay in a set-in bed,
The midwife threw my bundle away.

Here we dress up in a new grave,
The fish-boots with their herring scales
Inlaid as silver of a good week,
The jersey knitted close as nerves
Of the ground under the high bracken.
My eyes let light in on this dark.

When I fell from the hot to the cold
My father drew his whole day's pay,
My mother lay in a set-in bed,
The midwife threw my bundle away.

I, in Time's grace, the grace of change, sail surely
Moved off the land and the skilled keel sails
The darkness burning under where I go.
Landvoices and the lights ebb away
Raising the night round us. Unwinding whitely,
My changing motive pays me slowly out.
The sea sails in. The quay opens wide its arms
And waves us loose.

So I would have it, waved from home to out
After that, the continual other offer,
Intellect sung in a garment of innocence.
Here, formal and struck into a dead stillness,
The voyage sails you no more than your own.
And on its wrought epitaph fathers itself
The sea as metaphor of the sea. The boat
Rides in its fires.

And nursed now out on movement as we go,
Running white from the bow, the long keel sheathed
In departure leaving the sucked and slackening water
As mingled in memory; night rises stooped high over
Us as our boat keeps its nets and men and
Engraves its wake. Our bow heaves hung on a likely
Bearing for fish. The Mor Light flashes astern
Dead on its second.

Across our moving local of light the gulls
Go in a wailing slant. I watch, merged
In this and in a like event, as the boat
Takes the mild swell, and each event speaks through.
They speak me thoroughly to my faintest breath.
And for what sake? Each word is but a longing

Set out to break from a difficult home. Yet in
Its meaning I am.

The weather's come round. For us it's better broken.
Changed and shifted above us, the sky is broken
Now into a few light patches brightly ground
With its rough smithers and those swells lengthening
Easy on us, outride us in a slow follow
From stern to stem. The keel in its amorous furrow
Goes through each word. He drowns, who but ill
Resembled me.

In those words through which I move, leaving a cry
Formed in exact degree and set dead at
The mingling flood, I am put forward on to
Live water, clad in oil, burnt by salt
To life. Here, braced, announced on to the slow
Heaving seaboards, almost I am now too
Lulled. And my watch is blear. The early grey
Air is blowing.

It is that first pallor there, broken, running
Back on the sheared water. Now the chill wind
Comes off the shore sharp to find its old mark
Between the shoulderblades. My eyes read in
The fixed and flying signs wound in the light
Which all shall soon lie wound in as it slowly
Approaches rising to break wide up over the
Brow of the sea.

My need reads in light more specially gendered and
Ambitioned by all eyes that wide have been
Me once. The cross-tree light, yellowing now,
Swings clean across Orion. And waned and very
Gently the old signs tilt and somersault

Towards their home. The undertow, come hard round,
Now leans the tiller strongly jammed over
On my hip-bone.

It is us at last sailed into the chance
Of a good take. For there is the water gone
Lit black and wrought like iron into the look
That's right for herring. We dropped to the single motor.
The uneasy and roused gulls slid across us with
Swelled throats screeching. Our eyes sharpened what
Place we made through them. Now almost the light
To shoot the nets,

And keep a slow headway. One last check
To the gear. Our mended newtanned nets, all ropes
Loose and unkinked, tethers and springropes fast,
The tethers generous with floats to ride high,
And the big white bladder floats at hand to heave.
The bow wakes hardly a spark at the black hull.
The night and day both change their flesh about
In merging levels.

No more than merely leaning on the sea
We move. We move on this near-stillness enough
To keep the rudder live and gripped in the keel-wash.
We're well hinted herring plenty for the taking,
About as certain as all those signs falling
Through their appearance. Gulls settle lightly forward
Then scare off wailing as the sea-dusk lessens
Over our stern.

Yes, we're right set, see, see them go down, the best
Fishmarks, the gannets. They wheel high for a moment
Then heel, slip off the bearing air to plummet
Into the schooling sea. It's right for shooting,

Fish breaking the oiled water, the sea still
Holding its fires. Right, easy ahead, we'll run
Them straight out lined to the west. Now they go over,
White float and rope

And the net fed out in arm-lengths over the side.
So we shoot out the slowly diving nets
Like sowing grain. There they drag back their drifting
Weight out astern, a good half-mile of corks
And bladders. The last net's gone and we make fast
And cut the motor. The corks in a gentle wake,
Over curtains of water, tether us stopped, lapped
At far last still.

It is us no more moving, only the mere
Maintaining levels as they mingle together.
Now round the boat, drifting its drowning curtains
A grey of light begins. These words take place.
The petrel dips at the water-fats. And quietly
The stillness makes its way to its ultimate home.
The bilges slap. Gulls wail and settle.
It is us still.

At last it's all so still. We hull to the nets,
And rest back with our shoulders slacked pleasantly.
And I am illusioned out of this flood as
Separate and stopped to trace all grace arriving.
This grace, this movement bled into this place,
Locks the boat still in the grey of the seized sea.
The illuminations of innocence embrace.
What measures gently

Cross in the air to us to fix us so still
In this still brightness by knowledge of
The quick proportions of our intricacies?

What sudden perfection is this the measurement of?
And speaks us thoroughly to the bone and has
The iron sea engraved to our faintest breath,
The spray fretted and fixed at a high temper,
A script of light.

So I have been called by my name and
It was not sound. It is me named upon
The space which I continually move across
Bearing between my courage and my lack
The constant I bleed on. And, put to stillness,
Fixed in this metal and its cutting salts,
It is this instant to exact degree,
And for whose sake?

It is this instant written dead. This instant,
Bounded by its own grace and all Time's grace,
Masters me into its measurement so that
My ghostly constant is articulated.
Then suddenly like struck rock all points unfix.
The whole east breaks and leans at last to us,
Ancient overhead. Yet not a break of light
But mingles into

The whole memory of light, and will not cease
Contributing its exiled quality.
The great morning moves from its equivalent
Still where it lies struck in expressed proportion.
The streaming morning in its tensile light
Leans to us and looks over on the sea.
It's time to haul. The air stirs its faint pressures,
A slat of wind.

We are at the hauling then hoping for it
The hard slow haul of a net white with herring

Meshed hard. I haul, using the boat's cross-heave
We've started, holding fast as we rock back,
Taking slack as we go to. The day rises brighter
Over us and the gulls rise in a wailing scare
From the nearest net-floats. And the unfolding water
Mingles its dead.

Now better white I can say what's better sighted,
The white net flashing under the watched water,
The near net dragging back with the full belly
Of a good take certain, so drifted easy
Slow down on us or us hauled up upon it
Curved in a garment down to thicker fathoms.
The hauling nets come in sawing the gunwale
With herring scales.

The air bunches to a wind and roused sea-cries.
The weather moves and stoops high over us and
There the forked tern, where my look's whetted on distance,
Quarters its hunting sea. I haul slowly
Inboard the drowning flood as into memory,
Braced at the breathside in my net of nerves.
We haul and drift them home. The winds slowly
Turn round on us and

Gather towards us with dragging weights of water
Sleekly swelling across the humming sea
And gather heavier. We haul and hold and haul
Well the bright chirpers home, so drifted whitely
All a blinding garment out of the grey water.
And, hauling hard in the drag, the nets come in,
The headrope a sore pull and feeding its brine
Into our hacked hands.

Over the gunwale over into our deep lap
The herring come in, staring from their scales,
Fruitful as our deserts would have it out of
The deep and shifting seams of water. We haul
Against time fallen ill over the gathering
Rush of the sea together. The calms dive down.
The strident kingforked airs roar in their shell.
We haul the last

Net home and the last tether off the gathering
Run of the started sea. And then was the first
Hand at last lifted getting us swung against
Into the homing quarter, running that white grace
That sails me surely ever away from home.
And we hold into it as it moves down on
Us running white on the hull heeled to light.
Our bow heads home

Into the running blackbacks soaring us loud
High up in open arms of the towering sea.
The steep bow heaves, hung on these words, towards
What words your lonely breath blows out to meet it.
It is the skilled keel itself knowing its own
Fathoms it further moves through, with us there
Kept in its common timbers, yet each of us
Unwound upon

By a lonely behaviour of the all common ocean.
I cried headlong from my dead. The long rollers,
Quick on the crests and shirred with fine foam,
Surge down then sledge their green tons weighing dead
Down on the shuddered deck-boards. And shook off
All that white arrival upon us back to falter
Into the waking spoil and to be lost in
The mingling world.

So we were started back over that sea we
Had worked widely all fish-seasons and over
Its shifting grounds, yet now risen up into
Such humours, I felt like a farmer tricked to sea.
For it sailed sore against us. It grew up
To black banks that crossed us. It stooped, beaked.
Its brine burnt us. I was chosen and given.
It rose as risen

Treachery becomes myself, to clip me amorously
Off from all common breath. Those fires burned
Sprigs of the foam and branching tines of water.
It rose so white, soaring slowly, up
On us, then broke, down on us. It became a mull
Against our going and unfastened under us and
Curdled from the stern. It shipped us at each blow.
The brute weight

Of the living sea wrought us, yet the boat sleeked lean
Into it, upheld by the whole sea-brunt heaved,
And hung on the swivelling tops. The tiller raised
The siding tide to wrench us and took a good
Ready hand to hold it. Yet we made a seaway
And minded all the gear was fast, and took
Our spell at steering. And we went keeled over
The streaming sea.

See how, like an early self, it's loath to leave
And stares from the scuppers as it swirls away
To be clenched up. What a great width stretches
Farsighted away fighting in its white straits
On either bow, but bears up our boat on all
Its plaiting strands. This wedge driven in
To the twisting water, we rode. The bow shores
The long rollers.

The keel climbs and, with screws spinning out of their bite,
We drive down into the roar of the great doorways,
Each time almost to overstay, but start
Up into again the yelling gale and hailing
Shot of the spray. Yet we should have land
Soon marking us out of this thick distance and
How far we're in. Who is that poor sea-scholar,
Braced in his hero,

Lost in his book of storms there? It is myself.
So he who died is announced. This mingling element
Gives up myself. Words travel from what they once
Passed silence with. Here, in this intricate death,
He goes as fixed on silence as ever he'll be.
Leave him, nor cup a hand to shout him out
Of that, his home. Or, if you would, O surely
There is no word,

There is not any to go over that.
It is now as always this difficult air
We look towards each other through. And is there
Some singing look or word or gesture of grace
Or naked wide regard from the encountered face,
Goes ever true through the difficult air?
Each word speaks its own speaker to his death.
And we saw land

At last marked on the tenting mist and we could
Just make out the ridge running from the north
To the Black Rosses, and even mark the dark hint
Of Skeer well starboard. Now inside the bight
The sea was loosening and the screws spun steadier
Beneath us. We still shipped the blown water but
It broke white, not green weight caved in on us.
In out of all

That forming and breaking sea we came on the long
Swell close at last inshore with the day grey
With mewing distances and mist. The rocks rose
Waving their lazy friendly weed. We came in
Moving now by the world's side. And O the land lay
Just as we knew it well all along that shore
Akin to us with each of its dear seamarks. And lay
Like a mother.

We came in, riding steady in the bay water,
A sailing pillar of gulls, past the cockle strand.
And springing teal came out off the long sand. We
Moved under the soaring land sheathed in fair water
In that time's morning grace. I uttered that place
And left each word I was. The quay-heads lift up
To pass us in. These sea-worked measures end now.
And this element

Ends as we move off from its formal instant.
Now he who takes my place continually anew
Speaks me thoroughly perished into another.
And the quay opened its arms. I heard the sea
Close on him gently swinging on oiled hinges.
Moored here, we cut the motor quiet. He that
I'm not lies down. Men shout. Words break. I am
My fruitful share.

4

Only leaned at rest
Where my home is cast
Cannonwise on silence
And the serving distance.

O my love, keep the day
Leaned at rest, leaned at rest.

Only breathed at ease
In that loneliness
Bragged into a voyage
On the maintaining image.

O my love, there we lay
Loved alone, loved alone.

Only graced in my
Changing madman who
Sings but has no time
To divine my room.

O my love, keep the day
Leaned at rest, leaned at rest.

What one place remains
Home as darkness quickens?

5

So this is the place. This
Is the place fastened still with movement,
Movement as calligraphic and formal as
A music burned on copper.

At this place
The eye reads forward as the memory reads back.
At this last word all words change.
All words change in acknowledgement of the last.
Here is their mingling element.
This is myself (who but ill resembles me).
He befriended so many
Disguises to wander in on as many roads
As cross on a ball of wool.
What a stranger he's brought to pass

Who sits here in his place.
What a man arrived breathless
With a look or word to a few
Before he's off again.

Here is this place no more
Certain though the steep streets
And High Street form again and the sea
Swing shut on hinges and the doors all open wide.

6

As leaned at rest in lamplight with
The offered moth and heard breath
By grace of change serving my birth,

And as at hushed called by the owl,
With my chair up to my salt-scrubbed table,
While my endured walls kept me still,

I leaned and with a kind word gently
Struck the held air like a doorway
Bled open to meet another's eye.

Lie down, my recent madman, hardly
Drawn into breath than shed to memory,
For there you'll labour less lonely.

Lie down and serve. Your death is past.
There the fishing ground is richest.
There contribute your sleight of cast.

The rigged ship in its walls of glass
Still further forms its perfect seas
Locked in its past transparences.

You're come among somewhere the early
Children at play who govern my way
And shed each tear which burns my eye.

Thus, shed into the industrious grave
Ever of my life, you serve the love
Whose motive we are energies of.

So quietly my words upon the air
Awoke their harmonies for ever
Contending within the ear they alter.

And as the lamp burned back the silence
And the walls caved to a clear lens,
The room again became my distance.

I sat rested at the grave's table
Saying his epitaph who shall
Be after me to shout farewell.

7

Far out, faintly rocked,
Struck the sea bell.

Home becomes this place,
A bitter night, ill
To labour at dead of.
Within all the dead of
All my life I hear
My name spoken out
On the break of the surf.
I, in Time's grace,
The grace of change, am

Cast into memory.
What a restless grace
To trace stillness on.

Now this place about me
Wakes the night's twin shafts
And sheds the quay slowly.
Very gently the keel
Walks its waters again.
The sea awakes its fires.
White water stares in
From the harbour-mouth.
And we run through well
Held off the black land
Out into the waving
Nerves of the open sea.

My dead in the crew
Have mixed all qualities
That I have been and,
Though ghosted behind
My sides spurred by the spray,
Endure by a further gaze
Pearled behind my eyes.
Far out faintly calls
The mingling sea.

Now again blindfold
With the hemisphere
Unprised and bright
Ancient overhead,

This present place is
Become made into
A breathless still place

Unrolled on a scroll
And turned to face this light.

So I spoke and died.
So within the dead
Of night and the dead
Of all my life those
Words died and awoke.

from SEVEN LETTERS

LETTER II

Burned in this element
To the bare bone, I am
Trusted on the language.
I am to walk to you
Through the night and through
Each word you make between
Each word I burn bright in
On this wide reach. And you,
Within what arms you lie,
Hear my burning ways
Across these darknesses
That move and merge like foam.
Lie in the world's room,
My dear, and contribute
Here where all dialogues write.

Younger in the towered
Tenement of night he heard
The shipyards with nightshifts
Of lathes turning their shafts.
His voice was a humble ear
Hardly turned to her.
Then in a welding flash
He found his poetry arm
And turned the coat of his trade.
From where I am I hear
Clearly his heart beat over
Clydeside's far hammers
And the nightshipping firth.

What's he to me? Only
Myself I died from into
These present words that move.
In that high tenement
I got a great grave.

Tonight in sadly need
Of you I move inhuman
Across this space of dread
And silence in my mind.
I walk the dead water
Burning language towards
You where you lie in the dark
Ascension of all words.
Yet where? Where do you lie
Lost to my cry and hidden
Away from the world's downfall?
O offer some way tonight
To make your love take place
In every word. Reply.
Time's branches burn to hear.
Take heed. Reply. Here
I am driven burning on
This loneliest element. Break
Break me out of this night,
This silence where you are not,
Nor any within earshot.
Break break me from this high
Helmet of idiocy.

> Water water wallflower
> Growing up so high
> We are all children
> We all must die.
> Except Willie Graham

The fairest of them all.
He can dance and he can sing
And he can turn his face to the wall.
Fie, fie, fie for shame
Turn your face to the wall again.

Yes laugh then cloudily laugh
Though he sat there as deaf
And worn to a stop
As the word had given him up.
Stay still. That was the sounding
Sea he moved on burning
His still unending cry.
That night hammered and waved
Its starry shipyard arms,
And it came to inherit
His death where these words merge.
This is his night writ large.
In Greenock the bright breath
Of night's array shone forth
On the nightshifting town.
Thus younger burning in
The best of his puny gear
He early set out
To write him to this death
And to that great breath
Taking of the sea,
The graith of Poetry.
My musing love lie down
Within his arms. He dies
Word by each word into

Myself now at this last
Word I die in. This last.

A day the wind was hardly
Shaking the youngest frond
Of April I went on
The high moor we know.
I put my childhood out
Into a cocked hat
And you moving the myrtle
Walked slowly over.
A sweet clearness became.
The Clyde sleeved in its firth
Reached and dazzled me.
I moved and caught the sweet
Courtesy of your mouth.
My breath to your breath.
And as you lay fondly
In the crushed smell of the moor
The courageous and just sun
Opened its door.
And there we lay halfway
Your body and my body
On the high moor. Without
A word then we went
Our ways. I heard the moor
Curling its cries far
Across the still loch.

The great verbs of the sea
Come down on us in a roar.
What shall I answer for?

from TWO BALLADS

THE BROAD CLOSE

Come dodge the deathblow if you can
    Between a word or two.
Forget the times we've fallen out
    Or who we've fallen through.
For you are me all over again
    Except where you are new.

I may have hurled my skills away,
    Such as they are, but me,
Well, I'm jackeasy if I slip
    The muse a length for she
Appreciates the starkest man
    Her length and breadth to be.

But there you are. Grandfather whirrs
    And strikes dead on his time.
He was the rude oak of his day
    For the bluenose and the sperm
Till the midnight sun with a flensing spear
    Yelled and struck him dumb.

And there you were by Clydeside clad,
    Heir to a difficult home.
But here we fall as men alive
    Within this very room.
Read me your aid as the word falls
    Or all falls to bedlam.

'Twas on (or shall be on) a black
     Bitter Saturday night.
I sat broke in a black drouth
     And not a dram in sight.
I heard a homeward nightfaller
     Passing his courage out.

I think he was an old man
     By that dribbling pace.
And then he must have followed it
     And fell in the Broad Close,
And as he fell he jingled and
     I never heard him rise.

But that's all by the way. It was
     (As Meg was the first to find)
On such a night as would unman
     (It monkeyed with the gland.)
The best of us or even to freeze
     Them off a brass band.

I fell awake. My forty winks
     Fled as before a ghost.
I rose and looked out and the cobbles
     Looked in with a staring frost.
(Hang your coat on the first word.
     You lift it from the last).

They were my dead burning to catch
     Me up in a time to be.
To think they were once my joke and grief
     As real as this bad knee.
But now they are to the grave gone
     That's digged in memory.

The glass has blinded with a breath.
    All that sight is out.
Why should they stare from the grave again
    At me they died to meet?
The sweet oil walks within the wick
    And gulls on the shore bleat.

Away with them all! Now can you sing
    The Smashing of the Van?
You'll not be in your better form
    But I'm an easy man.
Just strike up one with a go and I'll
    Beat out the time till dawn.

O sing my grief as joke through
    All the sad counterparts.
Your voice is mine all over again,
    The voice of a lad of parts,
The voice out of the whisky bush,
    The reek in the breathless arts.

But stop. Allow me time to tell.
    The tongue on the quay told.
And told me it was time my great
    Inheritance was hauled.
(O never have heed of dead folk
    If you find them afield.)

I took my weapons up and went
    With hardly a word to spare.
And I wore my father's error for
    That I'll always wear.
But there was no bad in me
    As I went from that door.

And may he strike me down without
    The turn of a holy hair
If there was any bad in me
    When I went from that door.
And as I went my breath aghast
    Proceeded me before.

I tell it here upon the old
    Voices and the new,
And let them have their fling between
    Meanings out of the true
That they may make a harmony
    That's proper to us two.

And I went out on any word
    Would bring me to myself
And they were cold and hard words
    And cut my truth in half.
But I was blind till the frost blazed
    Me suddenly wakerife.

I heard the blindman's hedge and all
    The white roar of the sea.
I saw the deaf man's bell that struck
    The ice from off the tree.
And then I heard but a thin sound,
    Went straight to where he lay.

And O it is not to ask me by
    The flensing or the spear,
Or the grey table of the grave
    That writes between us here.
But it is enough to ask me by
    His likeness I wear.

'Come dodge the death blow, old man
　　For I see you are not fain
To yield me my inheritance,
　　But you will feel no pain.
You died to meet me once and now
　　You are to die again.

And cock your ears and leave no word
　　Unturned that I am in.
For the gale will skelp upon the firth
　　And drive the hailing stone,
And you out of the weather where
　　There is not flesh or bone.

If I am you all over again
　　By the joke and by the grief
Dodge if you can this very word,
　　For it is the flensing knife.'
And I have put it in his breast
　　And taken away his life.

I turned it round for all that
　　Seeing he did not stir.
And the Broad Close was bitter and
　　Is bitter at this hour.
The sweet oil walks within the wick
　　And gulls bleat on the shore.

Both wit and weapons must the king
　　Have over all alive
And over all his dead that they
　　Do him only love.
And wit and weapons must the king
　　Have down into the grave.

THE DARK INTENTION

My first intention was at least not this
That darkly gathers over the ground.
The dark discloses us in different ways.

Here in this wood can I be this disguise
Wielding a muffled light without a sound?
My first intention was at least not this.

This dark man strong in spades I have to face.
For I who hide and seek shall not be found.
The dark discloses us in different ways.

The wood is walking round me yet this place
Itself which I have made is still profound.
My first intention was at least not this.

What cracked that stick? Who made that black noise?
The dark is seeing what the blind astound.
The dark discloses us in different ways.

From dark to dark, aloneness to aloneness
I move and hope to move out of the round.
My first intention was at least not this.
The dark discloses us in different ways.

MALCOLM MOONEY'S LAND

1

Today, Tuesday, I decided to move on
Although the wind was veering. Better to move
Than have them at my heels, poor friends
I buried earlier under the printed snow.
From wherever it is I urge these words
To find their subtle vents, the northern dazzle
Of silence cranes to watch. Footprint on foot
Print, word on word and each on a fool's errand.
Malcolm Mooney's Land. Elizabeth
Was in my thoughts all morning and the boy.
Wherever I speak from or in what particular
Voice, this is always a record of me in you.
I can record at least out there to the west
The grinding bergs and, listen, further off
Where we are going, the glacier calves
Making its sudden momentary thunder.
This is as good a night, a place as any.

2

From the rimed bag of sleep, Wednesday,
My words crackle in the early air.
Thistles of ice about my chin,
My dreams, my breath a ruff of crystals.
The new ice falls from canvas walls.
O benign creature with the small ear-hole,
Submerger under silence, lead
Me where the unblubbered monster goes
Listening and makes his play.
Make my impediment mean no ill
And be itself a way.

A fox was here last night (Maybe Nansen's,
Reading my instruments.) the prints
All round the tent and not a sound.
Not that I'd have him call my name.
Anyhow how should he know? Enough
Voices are with me here and more
The further I go. Yesterday
I heard the telephone ringing deep
Down in a blue crevasse.
I did not answer it and could
Hardly bear to pass.

Landlice, always my good bedfellows,
Ride with me in my sweaty seams.
Come bonny friendly beasts, brother
To the grammarsow and the word-louse,
Bite me your presence, keep me awake
In the cold with work to do, to remember
To put down something to take back.
I have reached the edge of earshot here
And by the laws of distance
My words go through the smoking air
Changing their tune on silence.

3

My friend who loves owls
Has been with me all day
Walking at my ear
And speaking of old summers
When to speak was easy.
His eyes are almost gone
Which made him hear well.
Under our feet the great
Glacier drove its keel.
What is to read there

Scored out in the dark?
Later the north-west distance
Thickened towards us.
The blizzard grew and proved
Too filled with other voices
High and desperate
For me to hear him more.
I turned to see him go
Becoming shapeless into
The shrill swerving snow.

4

Today, Friday, holds the white
Paper up too close to see
Me here in a white-out in this tent of a place
And why is it there has to be
Some place to find, however momentarily
To speak from, some distance to listen to?

Out at the far-off edge I hear
Colliding voices, drifted, yes
To find me through the slowly opening leads.
Tomorrow I'll try the rafted ice.
Have I not been trying to use the obstacle
Of language well? It freezes round us all.

5

Why did you choose this place
For us to meet? Sit
With me between this word
And this, my furry queen.
Yet not mistake this
For the real thing. Here
In Malcolm Mooney's Land

I have heard many
Approachers in the distance
Shouting. Early hunters
Skittering across the ice
Full of enthusiasm
And making fly and,
Within the ear, the yelling
Spear steepening to
The real prey, the right
Prey of the moment.
The honking choir in fear
Leave the tilting floe
And enter the sliding water.
Above the bergs the foolish
Voices are lighting lamps
And all their sounds make
This diary of a place
Writing us both in.

Come and sit. Or is
It right to stay here
While, outside the tent
The bearded blinded go
Calming their children
Into the ovens of frost?
And what's the news? What
Brought you here through
The spring leads opening?

Elizabeth, you and the boy
Have been with me often
Especially on those last
Stages. Tell him a story.
Tell him I came across
An old sulphur bear

Sawing his log of sleep
Loud beneath the snow.
He puffed the powdered light
Up on to this page
And here his reek fell
In splinters among
These words. He snored well.
Elizabeth, my furry
Pelted queen of Malcolm
Mooney's Land, I made
You here beside me
For a moment out
Of the correct fatigue.

I have made myself alone now.
Outside the tent endless
Drifting hummock crests.
Words drifting on words.
The real unabstract snow.

THE BEAST IN THE SPACE

Shut up. Shut up. There's nobody here.
If you think you hear somebody knocking
On the other side of the words, pay
No attention. It will be only
The great creature that thumps its tail
On silence on the other side.
If you do not even hear that
I'll give the beast a quick skelp
And through Art you'll hear it yelp.

The beast that lives on silence takes
Its bite out of either side.
It pads and sniffs between us. Now
It comes and laps my meaning up.
Call it over. Call it across
This curious necessary space.
Get off, you terrible inhabiter
Of silence. I'll not have it. Get
Away to whoever it is will have you.

He's gone and if he's gone to you
That's fair enough. For on this side
Of the words it's late. The heavy moth
Bangs on the pane. The whole house
Is sleeping and I remember
I am not here, only the space
I sent the terrible beast across.
Watch. He bites. Listen gently
To any song he snorts or growls
And give him food. He means neither
Well or ill towards you. Above
All, shut up. Give him your love.

THE CONSTRUCTED SPACE

Meanwhile surely there must be something to say,
Maybe not suitable but at least happy
In a sense here between us two whoever
We are. Anyhow here we are and never
Before have we two faced each other who face
Each other now across this abstract scene
Stretching between us. This is a public place
Achieved against subjective odds and then
Mainly an obstacle to what I mean.

It is like that, remember. It is like that
Very often at the beginning till we are met
By some intention risen up out of nothing.
And even then we know what we are saying
Only when it is said and fixed and dead.
Or maybe, surely, of course we never know
What we have said, what lonely meanings are read
Into the space we make. And yet I say
This silence here for in it I might hear you.

I say this silence or, better, construct this space
So that somehow something may move across
The caught habits of language to you and me.
From where we are it is not us we see
And times are hastening yet, disguise is mortal.
The times continually disclose our home.
Here in the present tense disguise is mortal.
The trying times are hastening. Yet here I am
More truly now this abstract act become.

THE THERMAL STAIR

For the painter Peter Lanyon killed in a gliding accident 1964

I called today, Peter, and you were away.
I look out over Botallack and over Ding
Dong and Levant and over the jasper sea.

Find me a thermal to speak and soar to you from
Over Lanyon Quoit and the circling stones standing
High on the moor over Gurnard's Head where some

Time three foxglove summers ago, you came.
The days are shortening over Little Parc Owles.
The poet or painter steers his life to maim

Himself somehow for the job. His job is Love
Imagined into words or paint to make
An object that will stand and will not move.

Peter, I called and you were away, speaking
Only through what you made and at your best.
Look, there above Botallack, the buzzard riding

The salt updraught slides off the broken air
And out of sight to quarter a new place.
The Celtic sea, the Methodist sea is there.

> You said once in the Engine
> House below Morvah
> That words make their world
> In the same way as the painter's
> Mark surprises him
> Into seeing new.

Sit here on the sparstone
In this ruin where
Once the early beam
Engine pounded and broke
The air with industry.

Now the chuck of daws
And the listening sea.

'Shall we go down' you said
'Before the light goes
And stand under the old
Tinworkings around
Morvah and St Just?'
You said 'Here is the sea
Made by alfred wallis
Or any poet or painter's
Eye it encountered.
Or is it better made
By all those vesselled men
Sometime it maintained?
We all make it again.'

Give me your hand, Peter,
To steady me on the word.

Seventy-two by sixty,
Italy hangs on the wall.
A woman stands with a drink
In some polite place
And looks at SARACINESCO
And turns to mention space.
That one if she could
Would ride Artistically
The thermals you once rode.

Peter, the phallic boys
Begin to wink their lights.
Godrevy and the Wolf
Are calling Opening Time.
We'll take the quickest way
The tin singers made.
Climb here where the hand
Will not grasp on air.
And that dark-suited man
Has set the dominoes out
On the Queen's table.
Peter, we'll sit and drink
And go in the sea's roar
To Labrador with wallis
Or rise on Lanyon's stair.

Uneasy, lovable man, give me your painting
Hand to steady me taking the word-road home.
Lanyon, why is it you're earlier away?
Remember me wherever you listen from.
Lanyon, dingdong dingdong from carn to carn.
It seems tonight all Closing bells are tolling
Across the Duchy shire wherever I turn.

I LEAVE THIS AT YOUR EAR

For Nessie Dunsmuir

I leave this at your ear for when you wake,
A creature in its abstract cage asleep.
Your dreams blindfold you by the light they make.

The owl called from the naked-woman tree
As I came down by the Kyle farm to hear
Your house silent by the speaking sea.

I have come late but I have come before
Later with slaked steps from stone to stone
To hope to find you listening for the door.

I stand in the ticking room. My dear, I take
A moth kiss from your breath. The shore gulls cry.
I leave this at your ear for when you wake.

1

I always meant to only
Language swings away
Further before me.

Language swings away
Before me as I go
With again the night rising
Up to accompany me
And that other fond
Metaphor, the sea.
Images of night
And the sea changing
Should know me well enough.

Wanton with riding lights
And staring eyes, Europa
And her high meadow bull
Fall slowly their way
Behind the blindfold and
Across this more or less
Uncommon place.

And who are you and by
What right do I waylay
You where you go there
Happy enough striking
Your hobnail in the dark?
Believe me I would ask
Forgiveness but who
Would I ask forgiveness from?

I speak across the vast
Dialogues in which we go
To clench my words against
Time or the lack of time
Hoping that for a moment
They will become for me
A place I can think in
And think anything in,
An aside from the monstrous.

And this is no other
Place than where I am,
Here turning between
This word and the next.
Yet somewhere the stones
Are wagging in the dark
And you, whoever you are,
That I am other to,
Stand still by the glint
Of the dyke's sparstone,
Because always language
Is where the people are.

2

Almost I, yes, I hear
Huge in the small hours
A man's step on the stair
Climbing the pipeclayed flights
And then stop still
Under the stairhead gas
At the lonely tenement top.
The broken mantle roars
Or dims to a green murmur.
One door faces another.
Here, this is the door

With the loud grain and the name
Unreadable in brass.
Knock, but a small knock,
The children are asleep.
I sit here at the fire
And the children are there
And in this poem I am,
Whoever elsewhere I am,
Their mother through his mother.
I sit with the gas turned
Down and time knocking
Somewhere through the wall.
Wheesht, children, and sleep
As I break the raker up,
It is only the stranger
Hissing in the grate.
Only to speak and say
Something, little enough,
Not out of want
Nor out of love, to say
Something and to hear
That someone has heard me.
This is the house I married
Into, a room and kitchen
In a grey tenement,
The top flat of the land,
And I hear them breathe and turn
Over in their sleep
As I sit here becoming
Hardly who I know.
I have seen them hide
And seek and cry come out
Come out whoever you are
You're not het I called
And called across the wide

Wapenschaw of water.
But the place moved away
Beyond the reach of any
Word. Only the dark
Dialogues drew their breath.
Ah how bright the mantel
Brass shines over me.
Black-lead at my elbow,
Pipe-clay at my feet.
Wheesht and go to sleep
And grow up but not
To say mother mother
Where are the great games
I grew up quick to play.

3

Now in the third voice
I am their father through
Nothing more than where
I am made by this word
And this word to occur.
Here I am makeshift made
By artifice to fall
Upon a makeshift time.
But I can't see. I can't
See in the bad light
Moving (Is it moving?)
Between your eye and mine.
Who are you and yet
It doesn't matter only
I thought I heard somewhere
Someone else walking.
Where are the others? Why,
If there is any other,
Have they gone so far ahead?

Here where I am held
With the old rainy oak
And Cartsburn and the Otter's
Burn aroar in the dark
I try to pay for my keep.
I speak as well as I can
Trying to teach my ears
To learn to use their eyes
Even only maybe
In the end to observe
The behaviour of silence.
Who is it and why
Do you walk here so late
And how should you know to take
The left or the right fork
Or the way where, as a boy
I used to lie crouched
Deep under the flailing
Boughs of the roaring wood?
Or I lay still
Listening while a branch
Squeaked in the resinous dark
And swaying silences.

Otherwise I go
Only as a shell
Of my former self.
I go with my foot feeling
To find the side of the road,
My head inclined, my ears
Feathered to every wind
Blown between the dykes.
The mist is coming home.
I hear the blind horn
Mourning from the firth.

The big wind blows
Over the shore of my child
Hood in the off-season.
The small wind remurmurs
The fathering tenement
And a boy I knew running
The hide and seeking streets.
Or do these winds
In their forces blow
Between the words only?

I am the shell held
To Time's ear and you
May hear the lonely leagues
Of the kittiwake and the fulmar.

4

Or I am always only
Thinking is this the time
To look elsewhere to turn
Towards what was it
I put myself out
Away from home to meet?
Was it this only? Surely
It is more than these words
See on my side
I went halfway to meet.

And there are other times.
But the times are always
Other and now what I meant
To say or hear or be
Lies hidden where exile
Too easily beckons.
What if the terrible times

Moving away find
Me in the end only
Staying where I am always
Unheard by a fault.

So to begin to return
At last neither early
Nor late and go my way
Somehow home across
This gesture become
Inhabited out of hand.
I stop and listen over
My shoulder and listen back
On language for that step
That seems to fall after
My own step in the dark.

Always must be the lost
Or where we turn, and all
For a sight of the dark again.
The farthest away, the least
To answer back come nearest.

And this place is taking
Its time from us though these
Two people or voices
Are not us nor has
The time they seem to move in
To do with what we think
Our own times are. Even
Where they are is only
This one inhuman place.
Yet somewhere a stone
Speaks and maybe a leaf
In the dark turns over.

And whoever I meant
To think I had met
Turns away further
Before me blinded by
This word and this word.

See how presently
The bull and the girl turn
From what they seemed to say,
And turn there above me
With that star-plotted head
Snorting on silence.
The legend turns. And on
Her starry face descried
Faintly astonishment.
The formal meadow fades
Over the ever-widening
Firth and in their time
That not unnatural pair
Turn slowly home.

This is no other place
Than where I am, between
This word and the next.
Maybe I should expect
To find myself only
Saying that again
Here now at the end.
Yet over the great
Gantries and cantilevers
Of love, a sky, real and
Particular is slowly
Startled into light.

APPROACHES TO HOW THEY BEHAVE

1

What does it matter if the words
I choose, in the order I choose them in,
Go out into a silence I know
Nothing about, there to be let
In and entertained and charmed
Out of their master's orders? And yet
I would like to see where they go
And how without me they behave.

2

Speaking is difficult and one tries
To be exact and yet not to
Exact the prime intention to death.
On the other hand the appearance of things
Must not be made to mean another
Thing. It is a kind of triumph
To see them and to put them down
As what they are. The inadequacy
Of the living, animal language drives
Us all to metaphor and an attempt
To organise the spaces we think
We have made occur between the words.

3

The bad word and the bad word and
The word which glamours me with some
Quick face it pulls to make me let
It leave me to go across
In roughly your direction, hates

To go out maybe so completely
On another silence not its own.

4

Before I know it they are out
Afloat in the head which freezes them.
Then I suppose I take the best
Away and leave the others arranged
Like floating bergs to sink a convoy.

5

One word says to its mate O
I do not think we go together
Are we doing any good here
Why do we find ourselves put down?
The mate pleased to be spoken to
Looks up from the line below
And says well that doubtful god
Who has us here is far from sure
How we on our own tickle the chin
Of the prince or the dame that lets us in.

6

The dark companion is a star
Very present like a dark poem
Far and unreadable just out
At the edge of this poem floating.
It is not more or less a dark
Companion poem to the poem.

7

Language is expensive if
We want to strut, busked out
Showing our best on silence.

Good Morning. That is a bonny doing
Of verbs you wear with the celandine
Catching the same sun as mine.
You wear your dress like a prince but
A country's prince beyond my ken.
Through the chinks in your lyric coat
My ear catches a royal glimpse
Of fuzzed flesh, unworded body.
Was there something you wanted to say?
I myself dress up in what I can
Afford on the broadway. Underneath
My overcoat of the time's slang
I am fashionable enough wearing
The grave-clothes of my generous masters.

8

And what are you supposed to say
I asked a new word but it kept mum.
I had secretly admired always
What I thought it was here for.
But I was wrong when I looked it up
Between the painted boards. It said
Something it was never very likely
I could fit in to a poem in my life.

9

The good word said I am not pressed
For time. I have all the foxglove day
And all my user's days to give
You my attention. Shines the red
Fox in the digitalis grove.
Choose me choose me. Guess which
Word I am here calling myself
The best. If you can't fit me in

To lying down here among the fox
Glove towers of the moment, say
I am yours the more you use me. Tomorrow
Same place same time give me a ring.

10

Backwards the poem's just as good.
We human angels as we read
Read back as we gobble the words up.
Allowing the poem to represent
A recognizable landscape
Sprouting green up or letting green
With all its weight of love hang
To gravity's sweet affection,
Arse-versa it is the same object,
Even although the last word seems
To have sung first, or the breakfast lark
Sings up from the bottom of the sea.

11

The poem is not a string of knots
Tied for a meaning of another time
And country, unreadable, found
By chance. The poem is not a henge
Or Easter Island emerged Longnose
Or a tally used by early unknown
Peoples. The words we breathe and puff
Are our utensils down the dream
Into the manhole. Replace the cover.

12

The words are mine. The thoughts are all
Yours as they occur behind
The bat of your vast unseen eyes.

These words are as you see them put
Down on the dead-still page. They have
No ability above their station.
Their station on silence is exact.
What you do with them is nobody's business.

13

Running across the language lightly
This morning in the hangingover
Whistling light from the window, I
Was tripped and caught into the whole
Formal scheme which Art is.
I had only meant to enjoy
Dallying between the imaginary
And imaginary's opposite
With a thought or two up my sleeve.

14

Is the word? Yes Yes. But I hear
A sound without words from another
Person I can't see at my elbow.
A sigh to be proud of. You? Me?

15

Having to construct the silence first
To speak out on I realise
The silence even itself floats
At my ear-side with a character
I have not met before. Hello
Hello I shout but that silence
Floats steady, will not be marked
By an off-hand shout. For some reason
It refuses to be broken now
By what I thought was worth saying.

If I wait a while, if I look out
At the heavy greedy rooks on the wall
It will disperse. Now I construct
A new silence I hope to break.

CLUSTERS TRAVELLING OUT

1

Clearly I tap to you clearly
Along the plumbing of the world
I do not know enough, not
Knowing where it ends. I tap
And tap to interrupt silence into
Manmade durations making for this
Moment a dialect for our purpose.
TAPTAP. Are you reading that taptap
I send out to you along
My element? O watch. Here they come
Opening and shutting Communication's
Gates as they approach, History's
Princes with canisters of gas
Crystals to tip and snuff me out
Strangled and knotted with my kind
Under the terrible benevolent roof.

Clearly they try to frighten me
To almost death. I am presuming
You know who I am. To answer please
Tap tap quickly along the nearest
Metal. When you hear from me
Again I will not know you. Whoever
Speaks to you will not be me.
I wonder what I will say.

2

Remember I am here O not else
Where in this quick disguise, this very
Thought that's yours for a moment. I sit

Here behind this tempered mesh.
I think I hear you hearing me.
I think I see you seeing me.
I suppose I am really only about
Two feet away. You must excuse
Me, have I spoken to you before?
I seem to know your face from some
One else I was, that particular
Shadow head on the other side
Of the wire in the VISITORS ROOM.

I am learning to speak here in a way
Which may be useful afterwards.
Slops in hand we shuffle together,
Something to look forward to
Behind the spyhole. Here in our concrete
Soundbox we slide the jargon across
The watching air, a lipless language
Necessarily squashed from the side
To make its point against the rules.
It is our poetry such as it is.

Are you receiving those clusters
I send out travelling? Alas
I have no way of knowing or
If I am overheard here.
Is that (It is.) not what I want?

The slaughterhouse is next door.
Destroy this. They are very strict.

3

Can you see my As and Ys semaphore
Against the afterglow on the slaughterhouse

Roof where I stand on the black ridge
Waving my flagging arms to speak?

4

Corridors have their character. I know well
The ring of government boots on our concrete.
Malcolm's gone now. There's nobody to shout to.
But when they're not about in the morning I shout
HOY HOY HOY and the whole corridor rings
And I listen while my last HOY turns the elbow
With a fading surprised difference of tone and loses
Heart and in dwindling echoes vanishes away.
Each person who comes, their purpose precedes them
In how they walk. You learn to read that.
Sometimes the step's accompanied by metal
Jingling and metrical, filled with invention.
Metal opened and slammed is frightening. I try
To not be the first to speak. There is nothing to say.
Burn this. I do not dislike this place. I like
Being here. They are very kind. It's doing me good.

5

If this place I write from is real then
I must be allegorical. Or maybe
The place and myself are both the one
Side of the allegory and the other
Side is apart and still escaped
Outside. And where do you come in
With your musical key-ring and brilliant
Whistle pitched for the whipped dog?

And stands loving to recover me,
Lobe-skewers clipped to his swelling breast,
His humane-killer draped with a badged

Towel white as snow. And listen,
Ventriloquised for love his words
Gainsay any deep anguish left
For the human animal. O dear night
Cover up my beastly head.

6

Take note of who stands at my elbow listening
To all I say but not to all you hear.
She comes on Wednesdays, just on Wednesdays,
And today I make a Wednesday. On and off
I decide to make her my half-cousin Brigit
Back from the wrack and shingle on the Long Loch.
You yourself need pretend nothing. She
Is only here as an agent. She could not
On her own carry a message to you either
Written or dreamed by word of her perfect mouth.

Look. Because my words are stern and frown
She is somewhere wounded. She goes away. You see
It hasn't been a good Wednesday for her. For you
Has it been a good Wednesday? Or is yours Tuesday?

7

When the birds blow like burnt paper
Over the poorhouse roof and the slaughter
House and all the houses of Madron,
I would like to be out of myself and
About the extra, ordinary world
No matter what disguise it wears
For my sake, in my love.

It would be better than beside the Dnieper,
The Brahmaputra or a green daughter
Tributary of the Amazon.

But first I must empty my shit-bucket
And hope my case (if it can be found)
Will come up soon. I thought I heard
My name whispered on the vine.

Surrounded by howls the double-shifting
Slaughterhouse walls me in. High
On the wall I have my blue square
Through which I see the London–Cairo
Route floating like distant feathers.

I hear their freezing whistles. Reply
Carefully. They are cracking down.
Don't hurry away, I am waiting for
A message to come in now.

THE GREENOCK DIALOGUES

I

O Greenock, Greenock, I never will
Get back to you. But here I am,
The boy made good into a ghost
Which I will send along your streets
Tonight as the busy nightshifts
Hammer and spark their welding lights.

I pull this skiff I made myself
Across the almost midnight firth
Between Greenock and Kilkreggan.
My blades as they feather discard
The bright drops and the poor word
Which will always drown unheard.

Ah the little whirlpools go
Curling away for a moment back
Into my wake. Brigit. Cousin
Brigit Mooney, are you still there
On the Old Custom House shore?
You need not answer that, my dear.

And she is there with all the wisps
And murmurs in their far disguise.
Brigit, help with the boat up
Up over the shingle to the high
Tide mark. You've hardly changed, only
A little through the word's eye.

Take my hand this new night
And we'll go up to Cartsburn Street.

My poor father frightened to go
Down the manhole might be in.
Burns' Mary sleeps fine in
Inverkip Street far from Afton.

And here's the close, Brigit. My mother
Did those stairs a thousand times.
The top-flat door, my father's name
Scrived by his own hand in brass.
We stand here scrived on the silence
Under the hissing stairhead gas.

II

I (Who shall I be?) call across
The shore-side where like iron filings
The beasts of the tide are taken through
Their slow whirls between the words.
Where are you now, dear half-cousin
Brigit with your sandprints filling
In the Western, oystercatching morning?

This is a real place as far
As I am concerned. Come down over
The high-tide bladder-wrack and step
Over the gunwale of our good skiff.
I lean back on the bright blades
To move us out on language over
The loch in the morning, iodine air.

Abstract beasts in a morning mirror
By memory teased very far
Out of their origins. Where where
Shall I take us as the little whirl
Pools leave the blade and die back?

The house is shrinking. Yeats' hazel
Wood writes in a dwindling style.

From where I pull and feather I see
You dearly pulled towards me yet
Not moving nearer as we both
Move out over the burnished loch.
Move with the boat and keep us trim.
If it is a love we have, then it
Is only making it now, Brigit.

III

I am not trying to hide
Anything anything anything.
My half-cousin Brigit
With me rowed over the loch
And we pulled the skiff up
Up over the bladder
Wrack of the high tide
And climbed the Soor Duik ladder.

Ben Narnain is as good
A shape as any Ben
And I liked Ben Narnain
And half-cousin Brigit.
Remember she was only half
A cousin and not het.
These words play us both
About that time yet.

All this is far too
Innocently said.
I write this down to get her
Somewhere between the words.
You yourself can contribute

Somewhere between the words
If it does you any good.
I know what I climb towards.

Is that not (Will you say?)
Is that not right, Brigit?
With your naked feet printing
The oystercatching sand?
Shall I come back to Scotland,
My ear seeking the sound
Of what your words on the long
Loch have put in my mind.

After the bracken the open
Bare scree and the water
Ouzel and looking down
At the long loch. It was
I suppose fine but nothing
Now as the wind blows
Across the edge of Narnain
And the Soor Duik burn flows.

IV

There are various ways to try to speak
And this is one. Cousin Brigit,
Sit steady. Keep us trim
And I will pull us out over
The early morning firth between
Kilkreggan and Greenock. I'll put my blades
Easily with all my sleight into
My home waters not to distort
The surface from its natural sound.

Behind your head, where I can see,
The sleeping warrior lies along

The Arran hills. Steady, Brigit,
If you would ride the clinkered skiff
And see the little whirlpools scooped
Into their quick life and go
Sailing away astern. O help
To keep me headed into the fair
And loud forest of high derricks
And welding lights blue in the sun.

Whoever you are you are; keep
Us trimmed and easy as we go
Gliding at each stroke through
The oily shipbuilding approaches.
We are here to listen. We are here
To hear the town in the disguise
My memory puts on it. Brigit
Is with me. Her I know. I put
Her in between the lines to love
And be alive in particulars.

Brigit, dear broken-song-tongued bag,
I'll not be jilted again. I see
You younger now this morning, urged
Towards me as I put my back
Into the oars and as I lean
Towards you feathering the dripping blades,
I think almost you are more mine
Than his who was before. Remember
Your name is Brigit Mooney, kin
To Malcolm in his slowly moving
Ultramarine cell of ice.

Brigit, take me with you and who
Ever it is who reads himself into
Our presence here in this doubtful

Curious gesture. Come, step over
The gunwale. I think, it seems we're here
On the dirty pebbles of my home
Town Greenock where somewhere Burns' Mary
Sleeps and John Galt's ghosts go
Still in the annals of their parish.

WHAT IS THE LANGUAGE USING US FOR?

FIRST POEM

What is the language using us for?
Said Malcolm Mooney moving away
Slowly over the white language.
Where am I going said Malcolm Mooney.

Certain experiences seem to not
Want to go in to language maybe
Because of shame or the reader's shame.
Let us observe Malcolm Mooney.

Let us get through the suburbs and drive
Out further just for fun to see
What he will do. Reader, it does
Not matter. He is only going to be

Myself and for you slightly you
Wanting to be another. He fell
He falls (Tenses are everywhere.)
Deep down into a glass jail.

I am in a telephoneless, blue
Green crevasse and I can't get out.
I pay well for my messages
Being hoisted up when you are about.

I suppose you open them under the light
Of midnight of The Dancing Men.
The point is would you ever want
To be down here on the freezing line

Reading the words that steam out
Against the ice? Anyhow draw
This folded message up between
The leaning prisms from me below.

Slowly over the white language
Comes Malcolm Mooney the saviour.
My left leg has no feeling.
What is the language using us for?

SECOND POEM

1

What is the language using us for?
It uses us all and in its dark
Of dark actions selections differ.

I am not making a fool of myself
For you. What I am making is
A place for language in my life

Which I want to be a real place
Seeing I have to put up with it
Anyhow. What are Communication's

Mistakes in the magic medium doing
To us? It matters only in
So far as we want to be telling

Each other alive about each other
Alive. I want to be able to speak
And sing and make my soul occur

In front of the best and be respected
For that and even be understood
By the ones I like who are dead.

I would like to speak in front
Of myself with all my ears alive
And find out what it is I want.

2

What is the language using us for?
What shape of words shall put its arms
Round us for more than pleasure?

I met a man in Cartsburn Street
Thrown out of the Cartsburn Vaults.
He shouted Willie and I crossed the street

And met him at the mouth of the Close.
And this was double-breasted Sam,
A far relation on my mother's

West-Irish side. Hello Sam how
Was it you knew me and says he
I heard your voice on The Sweet Brown Knowe.

O was I now I said and Sam said
Maggie would have liked to see you.
I'll see you again I said and said

Sam I'll not keep you and turned
Away over the shortcut across
The midnight railway sidings.

What is the language using us for?
From the prevailing weather or words
Each object hides in a metaphor.

This is the morning. I am out
On a kind of Vlaminck blue-rutted
Road. Willie Wagtail is about.

In from the West a fine smirr
Of rain drifts across the hedge.
I am only out here to walk or

Make this poem up. The hill is
A shining blue macadam top.
I lean my back to the telegraph pole

And the messages hum through my spine.
The beaded wires with their birds
Above me are contacting London.

What is the language using us for?
It uses us all and in its dark
Of dark actions selections differ.

THIRD POEM

1

What is the language using us for?
The King of Whales dearly wanted
To have a word with me about how
I had behaved trying to crash
The Great Barrier. I could not speak
Or answer him easily in the white
Crystal of Art he set me in.

Who is the King of Whales? What is
He like? Well you may ask. He is
A kind of old uncle of mine
And yours mushing across the blind
Ice-cap between us in his furs
Shouting at his delinquent dogs.
What is his purpose? I try to find

Whatever it is is wanted by going
Out of my habits which is my name
To ask him how I can do better.
Tipped from a cake of ice I slid
Into the walrus-barking water
To find. I did not find another
At the end of my cold cry.

2

What is the language using us for?
The sailing men had sailing terms
Which rigged their inner-sailing thoughts
In forecastle and at home among
The kitchen of their kind. Tarry
Old Jack is taken aback at a blow
On the lubber of his domestic sea.

Sam, I had thought of going again
But it's no life. I signed on years
Ago and it wasn't the ship for me.
O leave 'er Johnny leave 'er.
Sam, what readers do we have aboard?
Only the one, Sir. Who is that?
Only myself, Sir, from Cartsburn Street.

3

What is the language using us for?
I don't know. Have the words ever
Made anything of you, near a kind
Of truth you thought you were? Me
Neither. The words like albatrosses
Are only a doubtful touch towards
My going and you lifting your hand

To speak to illustrate an observed
Catastrophe. What is the weather
Using us for where we are ready
With all our language lines aboard?
The beginning wind slaps the canvas.
Are you ready? Are you ready?

IMAGINE A FOREST

Imagine a forest
A real forest.

You are walking in it and it sighs
Round you where you go in a deep
Ballad on the border of a time
You have seemed to walk in before.
It is nightfall and you go through
Trying to find between the twittering
Shades the early starlight edge
Of the open moor land you know.
I have set you here and it is not a dream
I put you through. Go on between
The elephant bark of those beeches
Into that lightening, almost glade.

And he has taken
My word and gone

Through his own Ettrick darkening
Upon himself and he's come across
A glinted knight lying dying
On needles under a high tree.
Ease his visor open gently
To reveal whatever white, encased
Face will ask out at you who
It is you are or if you will
Finish him off. His eyes are open.
Imagine he does not speak. Only
His beard moving against the metal
Signs that he would like to speak.

Imagine a room
Where you are home

Taking your boots off from the wood
In that deep ballad very not
A dream and the fire noisily
Kindling up and breaking its sticks.
Do not imagine I put you there
For nothing. I put you through it
There in that holt of words between
The bearded liveoaks and the beeches
For you to meet a man alone
Slipping out of whatever cause
He thought he lay there dying for.

Hang up the ballad
Behind the door.

You are come home but you are about
To not fight hard enough and die
In a no less desolate dark wood
Where a stranger shall never enter.

Imagine a forest
A real forest.

ENTER A CLOUD

1

Gently disintegrate me
Said nothing at all.

Is there still time to say
Said I myself lying
In a bower of bramble
Into which I have fallen.

Look through my eyes up
At blue with not anything
We could have ever arranged
Slowly taking place.

Above the spires of the fox
Gloves and above the bracken
Tops with their young heads
Recognising the wind,
The armies of the empty
Blue press me further
Into Zennor Hill.

If I half-close my eyes
The spiked light leaps in
And I am here as near
Happy as I will get
In the sailing afternoon.

2

Enter a cloud. Between
The head of Zennor and

84

Gurnard's Head the long
Marine horizon makes
A blue wall or is it
A distant table-top
Of the far-off simple sea.

Enter a cloud. O cloud,
I see you entering from
Your west gathering yourself
Together into a white
Headlong. And now you move
And stream out of the Gurnard,
The west corner of my eye.

Enter a cloud. The cloud's
Changing shape is crossing
Slowly only an inch
Above the line of the sea.
Now nearly equidistant
Between Zennor and Gurnard's
Head, an elongated
White anvil is sailing
Not wanting to be a symbol.

3

Said nothing at all.

And proceeds with no idea
Of destination along
The sea bearing changing
Messages. Jean in London,
Lifting a cup, looking
Abstractedly out through
Her Hampstead glass will never
Be caught by your new shape

Above the chimneys. Jean,
Jean, do you not see
This cloud has been thought of
And written on Zennor Hill.

4

The cloud is going beyond
What I can see or make.
Over up-country maybe
Albert Strick stops and waves
Caught in the middle of teeling
Broccoli for the winter.
The cloud is not there yet.

From Gurnard's Head to Zennor
Head the level line
Crosses my eyes lying
On buzzing Zennor Hill.

The cloud is only a wisp
And gone behind the Head.
It is funny I got the sea's
Horizontal slightly surrealist.
Now when I raise myself
Out of the bracken I see
The long empty blue
Between the fishing Gurnard
And Zennor. It was a cloud
The language at my time's
Disposal made use of.

5

Thank you. And for your applause.
It has been a pleasure. I

Have never enjoyed speaking more.
May I also thank the real ones
Who have made this possible.
First, the cloud itself. And now
Gurnard's Head and Zennor
Head. Also recognise
How I have been helped
By Jean and Madron's Albert
Strick (He is a real man.)
And good words like brambles,
Bower, spiked, fox, anvil, teeling.

The bees you heard are from
A hive owned by my friend
Garfield down there below
In the house by Zennor Church.

The good blue sun is pressing
Me into Zennor Hill.

Gently disintegrate me
Said nothing at all.

GREENOCK AT NIGHT I FIND YOU

1

As for you loud Greenock long ropeworking
Hide and seeking rivetting town of my child
Hood, I know we think of us often mostly
At night. Have you ever desired me back
Into the set-in bed at the top of the land
In One Hope Street? I am myself lying
Half-asleep hearing the rivetting yards
And smelling the bone-works with no home
Work done for Cartsburn School in the morning.

At night. And here I am descending and
The welding lights in the shipyards flower blue
Under my hopeless eyelids as I lie
Sleeping conditioned to hide from happy.

2

So what did I do? I walked from Hope Street
Down Lyndoch Street between the night's words
To Cartsburn Street and got to the Cartsburn Vaults
With half an hour to go. See, I am back.

3

See, I am back. My father turned and I saw
He had the stick he cut in Sheelhill Glen.
Brigit was there and Hugh and double-breasted
Sam and Malcolm Mooney and Alastair Graham.
They all were there in the Cartsburn Vaults shining
To meet me but I was only remembered.

LOCH THOM

1

Just for the sake of recovering
I walked backward from fifty-six
Quick years of age wanting to see,
And managed not to trip or stumble
To find Loch Thom and turned round
To see the stretch of my childhood
Before me. Here is the loch. The same
Long-beaked cry curls across
The heather-edges of the water held
Between the hills a boyhood's walk
Up from Greenock. It is the morning.

And I am here with my mammy's
Bramble jam scones in my pocket.
The Firth is miles and I have come
Back to find Loch Thom maybe
In this light does not recognise me.

This is a lonely freshwater loch.
No farms on the edge. Only
Heather grouse-moor stretching
Down to Greenock and One Hope
Street or stretching away across
Into the blue moors of Ayrshire.

2

And almost I am back again
Wading the heather down to the edge
To sit. The minnows go by in shoals
Like iron filings in the shallows.

My mother is dead. My father is dead
And all the trout I used to know
Leaping from their sad rings are dead.

3

I drop my crumbs into the shallow
Weed for the minnows and pinheads.
You see that I will have to rise
And turn round and get back where
My running age will slow for a moment
To let me on. It is a colder
Stretch of water than I remember.

The curlew's cry travelling still
Kills me fairly. In front of me
The grouse flurry and settle. GOBACK
GOBACK GOBACK FAREWELL LOCH THOM.

TO ALEXANDER GRAHAM

Lying asleep walking
Last night I met my father
Who seemed pleased to see me.
He wanted to speak. I saw
His mouth saying something
But the dream had no sound.

We were surrounded by
Laid-up paddle steamers
In The Old Quay in Greenock.
I smelt the tar and the ropes.

It seemed that I was standing
Beside the big iron cannon
The tugs used to tie up to
When I was a boy. I turned
To see Dad standing just
Across the causeway under
That one lamp they keep on.

He recognised me immediately.
I could see that. He was
The handsome, same age
With his good brows as when
He would take me on Sundays
Saying we'll go for a walk.

Dad, what am I doing here?
What is it I am doing now?
Are you proud of me?
Going away, I knew
You wanted to tell me something.

You stopped and almost turned back
To say something. My father,
I try to be the best
In you you give me always.

Lying asleep turning
Round in the quay-lit dark
It was my father standing
As real as life. I smelt
The quay's tar and the ropes.

I think he wanted to speak.
But the dream had no sound.
I think I must have loved him.

JOHANN JOACHIM QUANTZ'S FIVE LESSONS

THE FIRST LESSON

So that each person may quickly find that
Which particularly concerns him, certain metaphors
Convenient to us within the compass of this
Lesson are to be allowed. It is best I sit
Here where I am to speak on the other side
Of language. You, of course, in your own time
And incident (I speak in the small hours.)
Will listen from your side. I am very pleased
We have sought us out. No doubt you have read
My Flute Book. Come. The Guild clock's iron men
Are striking out their few deserted hours
And here from my high window Brueghel's winter
Locks the canal below. I blow my fingers.

THE SECOND LESSON

Good morning, Karl. Sit down. I have been thinking
About your progress and my progress as one
Who teaches you, a young man with talent
And the rarer gift of application. I think
You must now be becoming a musician
Of a certain calibre. It is right maybe
That in our lessons now I should expect
Slight and very polite impatiences
To show in you. Karl, I think it is true,
You are now nearly able to play the flute.

Now we must try higher, aware of the terrible
Shapes of silence sitting outside your ear

Anxious to define you and really love you.
Remember silence is curious about its opposite
Element which you shall learn to represent.

Enough of that. Now stand in the correct position
So that the wood of the floor will come up through you.
Stand, but not too stiff. Keep your elbows down.
Now take a simple breath and make me a shape
Of clear unchained started and finished tones.
Karl, as well as you are able, stop
Your fingers into the breathing apertures
And speak and make the cylinder delight us.

THE THIRD LESSON

Karl, you are late. The traverse flute is not
A study to take lightly. I am cold waiting.
Put one piece of coal in the stove. This lesson
Shall not be prolonged. Right. Stand in your place.

Ready? Blow me a little ladder of sound
From a good stance so that you feel the heavy
Press of the floor coming up through you and
Keeping your pitch and tone in character.

Now that is something, Karl. You are getting on.
Unswell your head. One more piece of coal.
Go on now but remember it must be always
Easy and flowing. Light and shadow must
Be varied but be varied in your mind
Before you hear the eventual return sound.

Play me the dance you made for the barge-master.
Stop stop Karl. Play it as you first thought
Of it in the hot boat-kitchen. That is a pleasure

For me. I can see I am making you good.
Keep the stove red. Hand me the matches. Now
We can see better. Give me a shot at the pipe.
Karl, I can still put on a good flute-mouth
And show you in this high cold room something
You will be famous to have said you heard.

THE FOURTH LESSON

You are early this morning. What we have to do
Today is think of you as a little creator
After the big creator. And it can be argued
You are as necessary, even a composer
Composing in the flesh an attitude
To slay the ears of the gentry. Karl,
I know you find great joy in the great
Composers. But now you can put your lips to
The messages and blow them into sound
And enter and be there as well. You must
Be faithful to who you are speaking from
And yet it is all right. You will be there.

Take your coat off. Sit down. A glass of Bols
Will help us both. I think you are good enough
To not need me anymore. I think you know
You are not only an interpreter.
What you will do is always something else
And they will hear you simultaneously with
The Art you have been given to read. Karl,

I think the Spring is really coming at last.
I see the canal boys working. I realise
I have not asked you to play the flute today.
Come and look. Are the barges not moving?
You must forgive me. I am not myself today.

Be here on Thursday. When you come, bring
Me five herrings. Watch your fingers. Spring
Is apparent but it is still chilblain weather.

THE LAST LESSON

Dear Karl, this morning is our last lesson.
I have been given the opportunity to
Live in a certain person's house and tutor
Him and his daughters on the traverse flute.
Karl, you will be all right. In those recent
Lessons my heart lifted to your playing.

I know. I see you doing well, invited
In a great chamber in front of the gentry. I
Can see them with their dresses settling in
And bored mouths beneath moustaches sizing
You up as you are, a lout from the canal
With big ears but an angel's tread on the flute.

But you will be all right. Stand in your place
Before them. Remember Johann. Begin with good
Nerve and decision. Do not intrude too much
Into the message you carry and put out.

One last thing, Karl, remember when you enter
The joy of those quick high archipelagoes,
To make to keep your finger-stops as light
As feathers but definite. What can I say more?
Do not be sentimental or in your Art.
I will miss you. Do not expect applause.

LINES ON ROGER HILTON'S WATCH

Which I was given because
I loved him and we had
Terrible times together.

O tarnished ticking time
Piece with your bent hand,
You must be used to being
Looked at suddenly
In the middle of the night
When he switched the light on
Beside his bed. I hope
You told him the best time
When he lifted you up
To meet the Hilton gaze.

I lift you up from the mantel
Piece here in my house
Wearing your verdigris.
At least I keep you wound
And put my ear to you
To hear Botallack tick.

You realise your master
Has relinquished you
And gone to lie under
The ground at St Just.

Tell me the time. The time
Is Botallack o'clock.
This is the dead of night.

He switches the light on
To find a cigarette
And pours himself a Teachers.
He picks me up and holds me
Near his lonely face
To see my hands. He thinks
He is not being watched.

The images of his dream
Are still about his face
As he spits and tries not
To remember where he was.

I am only a watch
And pray time hastes away.
I think I am running down.

Watch, it is time I wound
You up again. I am
Very much not your dear
Last master but we had
Terrible times together.

IMPLEMENTS IN THEIR PLACES

1

Somewhere our belonging particles
Believe in us. If we could only find them.

2

Who calls? Don't fool me. Is it you
Or me or us in a faulty duet
Singing out of a glade in a wood
Which we would never really enter?

3

This time the muse in the guise
Of jailbait pressed against
That cheeky part of me which thinks
It likes to have its own way.
I put her out and made her change
Her coarse disguise but later she came
Into the room looking like an old
Tinopener and went to work on the company.

4

One night after punching the sexual
Clock I sat where I usually sit
Behind my barrier of propped words.
Who's there I shouted. And the face
Whitely flattened itself against
The black night-glass like a white pig
And entered and breathed beside me
Her rank breath of poet's bones.

5

When I was a buoy it seemed
Craft of rare tonnage
Moored to me. Now
Occasionally a skiff
Is tied to me and tugs
At the end of its tether.

6

He has been given a chair in that
Timeless University.
The Chair of Professor of Silence.

7

My father's ego sleeps in my bones
And wakens suddenly to find the son
With words dressed up to kill or at
The least maim for life another
Punter met in the betting yard.

8

He cocked his snoot, settled his cock,
Said goodbye darling to his darling,
Splurged on a taxi, recited the name
Of his host and wondered who would be there
Worthy of being his true self to.
They were out. It was the wrong night.
By underground he returned home
To his reading darling saying darling
Halfway there I realised the night
Would have been nothing without you there.

She stepped from the bath, interestedly
Dried herself not allowing herself
To feel or expect too much. She sat
Not naked doing her face thinking
I am a darling but what will they think
When I arrive without my darling.
Moving in her perfumed aura,
Her earrings making no sound,
She greets her hostess with a cheek-kiss
And dagger. Then disentangled
She babys her eyes and sends her gaze
Widening to wander through
The sipping archipelagoes
Of frantic islands. He was there
It was their night. Groomed again
She lets herself in at four with an oiled
Key thinking my handsome darling
Is better than me, able to pull
Our house and the children round him.

10

Out into across
The morning loch burnished
Between us goes the flat
Thrown poem and lands
Takes off and skips One
2, 3, 4, 5, 6, 7, 8, 9,
And ends and sinks under.

11

Mister Montgomerie. Mister Scop.
You, follicles. You, the owl.
Two famous men famous for far

Apart images. POLEEP POLEEP
The owl calls through the olive grove.
I come to her in a set-in bed
In a Greenock tenement. I see
The little circle of brown moles
Round her nipple. Good Montgomerie.

12

I could know you if I wanted to.
You make me not want to.
Why does everybody do that?

13

Down in a business well
In a canyon in lower Manhattan
I glanced up from the shades
To see old dye-haired Phoebus
Swerving appear in his gold
Souped-up convertible.

14

The greedy rooks. The Maw
Of the incongruous deep.
The appetite of the long
Barrelled gun of the sea.
The shrew's consumption.
And me abroad ahunting
Those distant morsels
Admired by man.

15

Raped by his colour slides her delighted
Pupils fondled their life together.

It was the fifty dirty milkbottles
Standing like an army turned their love sour.

16

Failures of love make their ghosts
Which float out from every object
The lovers respectively have ever
Sighed and been alive towards.

17

Sign me my right on the pillow of cloudy night.

18

In my task's husk a whisper said
Drop it It's bad It's bad anyhow.
Because I could not gracefully
Get out of what I was doing, I made
An inner task come to fruit
Invisible to all spectators.

19

The fine edge of the wave expects.
Ireland Scotland England expects.
He She They expect. My dear
Expects. And I am ready to see
How I should not expect to ever
Enfold her. But I do expect.

20

So sleeps and does not sleep
The little language of green glow
Worms by the wall where the mint sprouts.
The tails the tales of love are calling.

21

When you were younger and me hardly
Anything but who is in me still
I had a throat of loving for you
That I can hardly bear can bear.

22

I see it has fluttered to your hand
Drowned and singed. Can you read it?
It kills me. Why do you persist
In holding my message upsidedown?

23

Ho Ho Big West Prevailer,
Your beard brushes the gable
But tonight you make me sleep.

24

It is how one two three each word
Chose itself in its position
Pretending at the same time
They were working for me. Here
They are. Should I have sacked them?

25

At times a rare metaphor's
Fortuitous agents sing
Equally in their right.

26

Nouns are the very devil. Once
When the good nicely chosen verb
Came up which was to very do,

The king noun took the huff and changed
To represent another object.
I was embarrassed but I said something
Else and kept the extravert verb.

27

Only now a wordy ghost
Of once my firmer self I go
Floating across the frozen tundra
Of the lexicon and the dictionary.

28

Commuting by arterial words
Between my home and Cool Cat
Reality, I began to seem
To miss or not want to catch
My road to one or the other. Rimbaud
Knew what to do. Or Nansen letting
His world on the wooden Fram freeze in
To what was going to carry him.

29

These words as I uttered them
Spoke back at me out of spite,
Pretended to not know me
From Adam. Sad to have to infer
Such graft and treachery in the name
Of communication. O it's become
A circus of mountebanks, promiscuous
Highfliers, tantamount to wanting
To be servant to the more interesting angels.

30

Language, constrictor of my soul,
What are you snivelling at? Behave
Better. Take care. It's only through me
You live. Take care. Don't make me mad.

31

How are we doing not very well?
Perhaps the real message gets lost.
Or is it tampered with on the way
By the collective pain of Alive?

32

Member of Topside Jack's trades,
I tie my verse in a true reef
Fast for the purpose of joining.

33

Do not think you have to say
Anything back. But you do
Say something back which I
Hear by the way I speak to you.

34

As I hear so I speak so I am so I think
You must be. O Please Please No.

35

Language, you terrible surrounder
Of everything, what is the good
Of me isolating my few words
In a certain order to send them

Out in a suicide torpedo to hit?
I ride it. I will never know.

36

I movingly to you moving
Move on stillness I pretend
Is common ground forgetting not
Our sly irreconcilabilities.

37

Dammit these words are making faces
At me again. I hope the faces
They make at you have more love.

38

There must be a way to begin to try
Even to having to make up verse
Hoping that the poem's horned head
Looks up over the sad zoo railings
To roar whine bark in the characteristic
Gesture of its unique kind.
Come, my beast, there must be a way
To employ you as the whiskered Art
Object, or great Art-Eater
Licking your tongue into the hill.
The hunter in the language wood
Down wind is only after your skin.
Your food has stretched your neck too
Visible over the municipal hedge.
If I were you (which only I am)
I would not turn my high head
Even to me as your safe keeper.

39

Why should I hang around and yet
Whatever it is I want to say
Delays me. Am I greedier than you?
I linger on to hope to hear
The whale unsounding with a deep
Message about how I have behaved.
Down under in the indigo pressures
He counts the unsteady shriek of my pulse.

40

Kind me (O never never).
I leave you this space
To use as your own.
I think you will find
That using it is more
Impossible than making it.
Here is the space now.
Write an Implement in it.

YOU ....

YOU ....

YOU ....

YOU ....

Do it with your pen.
I will return in a moment
To see what you have done.
Try. Try. No offence meant.

41

I found her listed under Flora
Smudged on a coloured, shining plate
Dogeared and dirty. As for Fauna
We all are that, pelted with anarchy.

42

Your eyes glisten with wet spar.
My lamp dims in your breath. I want
I want out of this underword
But I can't turn round to crawl back.

43

Here now at the Poetry Face
My safety lamp names the muse Mineral.

44

Brushing off my hurts I came across
A thorn of Love deeply imbedded.
My wife lent me her eye-brow tweezers
And the little bad shaft emerged.
It is on the mantel-piece now but O
The ghost of the pain gives me gyp.

45

Tonight late alone, the only
Human awake in the house I go
Out in a foray into my mind
Armed with the language as I know it
To sword-dance in the halls of Angst.

46

By night a star-distinguisher
Looking up through the signed air.
By day an extinguisher of birds
Of silence caught in my impatient
Too-small-meshed poet's net.

47

Under his kilt his master
Led him to play the fool
Over the border and burn
A lady in her tower
In a loud lorry road
In tulipless Holland Park.

48

It is only when the tenant is gone
The shell speaks of the sea.

49

Knock knock. I knock on the drowned cabin
Boy's sea-chest. Yearning Corbiere
Eases up the lid to look out
And ask how is the sea today.

50

I dive to knock on the rusted, tight
Haspt locker of David Jones.
Who looks out? A mixed company.
Kandinsky's luminous worms,
Shelley, Crane and Melville and all
The rest. Who knows? Maybe even Eliot.

51

Hello. It's a pleasure. Is that a knowledge
You wear? You are dressed up today,
Brigit of early shallows of all
My early life wading in pools.
She lifts my words as a shell to hear
The Celtic wild waves learning English.

52

These words as they are (The beasts!)
Will never realise the upper
Hand is mine. They try to come
The tin-man with me. But now (I ask.)
Where do they think what do they think
They are now? The dear upstarts.

53

The word unblemished by the tongue
Of History has still to be got.
You see, Huntly, it is the way
You put it. Said Moray's Earl,
You've spoilt a bonnier face than your ain.
That's what he said when Huntly struck
The Scots iron into his face.

54

Officer myself, I had orders
To stay put, not to advance
On the enemy whose twigs of spring
Waved on their helmets as they less
Leadered than us deployed across
The other side of the ravine of silence.

55

From ventricle to ventricle
A sign of assumed love passes
To keep the organisation going.
Sometimes too hard sometimes too soft
I hear the night and the day mares
Galloping in the tenement top
In Greenock in my child brain.

56

Terrible the indignity of one's self flying
Away from the sleight of one's true hand.
Then it becomes me writing big
On the mirror and putting a moustache on myself.

57

There is no fifty-seven.
It is not here. Only
Freshwater Loch Thom
To paddle your feet in
And the long cry of the curlew.

58

Occasionally it is always night
Then who would hesitate to turn
To hope to see another face
Which is not one's own growing
Out of the heaving world's ship-wall?
From my bunk I prop myself
To look out through the salted glass
And see the school of black killers.
Grampus homes on the Graham tongue.

59

I've had enough said twig Ninety-thousand
Whispering across the swaying world
To twig Ninety-thousand-and-Fifty. This lack
Of communication takes all the sap
Out of me so far out. It is true.
They were on their own out at the edge
Changing their little live angles.
They were as much the tree as the trunk.
They were restless because the trunk

Seemed to never speak to them.
I think they were wrong. I carved my name
On the bark and went away hearing
The rustle of their high discussion.

60

I stand still and the wood marches
Towards me and divides towards
Me not to cover me up strangled
Under its ancient live anchors.
I stand in a ride now. And at
The meeting, dusk-filled end I see
(I wish I saw.) the shy move
Of the wood's god approaching to greet me.

61

You will observe that not one
Of those tree-trunks has our initials
Carved on it or heart or arrow
We could call ours. My dear, I think
We have come in to the wrong wood.

62

In Madron Wood the big cock rook
Says CHYUCK CHYUCK if I may speak
Here on behalf of our cock members,
This year we're building early and some
Of us have muses due to lay.

63

Feeding the dead is necessary.

64

I love you paralysed by me.
I love you made to lie. If you
Love me blink your right eye once.
If you don't love me blink your left.
Why do you flutter your just before
Dying dear two eyes at once?

65

Cretan girl in black, young early
Widow from stark Malia, please have
The last portion and let your mask
Go down on the handkerchief dancing floor.
It's me that's lost. Find me and put
Me into an octopus jar and let me
Be left for the young spectacled
Archaeologist sad in a distant womb.

66

I caught young Kipling in his pelmanic
Kimsgame scribbling on his cuff.
I found he was only counting the beasts
Of empire still abroad in the jungle.

67

Coming back to earth under my own
Name whispered by the under dear,
I extracted with care my dead right arm,
An urchin of pins and needles of love.

The earth was never flat. Always
The mind or earth wanderers' choice
Was up or down, a lonely vertical.

The long loch was not long enough.
The resident heron rose and went
That long length of water trailing
Its legs in air but couldn't make it.
He decided to stay then and devote
Himself to writing verse with his long
Beak in the shallows of the long loch-side.

(Is where you listen from becoming
Numb by the strike of the same key?)
It is our hazard. Heraklion, listen.

I can discern at a pinch you
Through the lens of the ouzo glass,
Your face globing this whole Piraeus
Taverna of buzzing plucked wires.
Here we are sitting, we two
In a very deep different country
At this table in the dark.
Inevitable tourists us,
Not in Scotland sitting here
In foreign shadows, bouzouki
Turning us into two others
Across the waiting eating table.
At home in Blantyre if your mother
Looked at the map with a microscope

Her Scotch palate would be appalled
To see us happy in the dark
Fishing the legs of creature eight
Out of the hot quink ink to eat.

72

I am not here. I am not here
At two o'clock in the morning just
For fun. I am not here for something.

73

Of air he knows nor does he speak
To earth. The day is sailing round
His heavenly wings. Daisies and cups
Of butter and dragonflies stop
Their meadow life to look up wondering
How out of what ridiculous season
The wingèd one descends.

74

Somewhere our belonging particles
Believe in us. If we could only find them.

DEAR BRYAN WYNTER

1

This is only a note
To say how sorry I am
You died. You will realise
What a position it puts
Me in. I couldn't really
Have died for you if so
I were inclined. The carn
Foxglove here on the wall
Outside your first house
Leans with me standing
In the Zennor wind.

Anyhow how are things?
Are you still somewhere
With your long legs
And twitching smile under
Your blue hat walking
Across a place? Or am
I greedy to make you up
Again out of memory?
Are you there at all?
I would like to think
You were all right
And not worried about
Monica and the children
And not unhappy or bored.

2

Speaking to you and not
Knowing if you are there

Is not too difficult.
My words are used to that.
Do you want anything?
Where shall I send something?
Rice-wine, meanders, paintings
By your contemporaries?
Or shall I send a kind
Of news of no time
Leaning against the wall
Outside your old house.

The house and the whole moor
Is flying in the mist.

3

I am up. I've washed
The front of my face
And here I stand looking
Out over the top
Half of my bedroom window.
There almost as far
As I can see I see
St Buryan's church tower.
An inch to the left, behind
That dark rise of woods,
Is where you used to lurk.

4

This is only a note
To say I am aware
You are not here. I find
It difficult to go
Beside Housman's star
Lit fences without you.

And nobody will laugh
At my jokes like you.

5

Bryan, I would be obliged
If you would scout things out
For me. Although I am not
Just ready to start out.
I am trying to be better,
Which will make you smile
Under your blue hat.

I know I make a symbol
Of the foxglove on the wall.
It is because it knows you.

TO MY WIFE AT MIDNIGHT

Are you to say goodnight
And turn away under
The blanket of your delight?

Are you to let me go
Alone to sleep beside you
Into the drifting snow?

Where we each reach,
Sleeping alone together,
Nobody can touch.

Is the cat's window open?
Shall I turn into your back?
And what is to happen?

What is to happen to us
And what is to happen to each
Of us asleep in our places?

I mean us both going
Into sleep at our ages
To sleep and get our fairing.

They have all gone home.
Night beasts are coming out.
The black wood of Madron

Is just waking up.
I hear the rain outside
To help me to go to sleep.

Nessie, dont let my soul
Skip and miss a beat
And cause me to fall.

3

Are you asleep I say
Into the back of your neck
For you not to hear me.

Are you asleep? I hear
Your heart under the pillow
Saying my dear my dear

My dear for all it's worth.
Where is the dun's moor
Which began your breath?

4

Ness, to tell you the truth
I am drifting away
Down to fish for the saithe.

Is the cat's window open?
The weather is on my shoulder
And I am drifting down

Into O can you hear me
Among your Dunsmuir Clan?
Are you coming out to play?

5

Did I behave badly
On the field at Culloden?
I lie sore-wounded now

By all activities, and
The terrible acts of my time
Are only a distant sound.

With responsibility
I am drifting off
Breathing regularly

Into my younger days
To play the games of Greenock
Beside the sugar-house quays.

6

Nessie Dunsmuir, I say
Wheesht wheesht to myself
To help me now to go

Under into somewhere
In the redcoat rain.
Buckle me for the war.

Are you to say goodnight
And kiss me and fasten
My drowsy armour tight?

My dear camp-follower,
Hap the blanket round me
And tuck in a flower.

Maybe from my sleep
In the stoure at Culloden
I'll see you here asleep

In your lonely place.

A WALK TO THE GULVAS

1

Ness, shall we go for a walk?
I'll take you up to the Gulvas
You never really got to.

Put on your lovely yellow
Oilskin to meet the weather.

2

This bit of the road, Ness,
We know well, is different
Continually. Macadam
Has not smoothed it to death.
When the light keeks out, the road
Answers and shines up blue.
I thought we might have seen
Willie Wagtail from earlier.
Nessie, how many steps
Do we take from pole to pole
Going up this hill? I see
Your Blantyre rainy lashes.
The five wires are humming
Every good boy deserves
Favour. We have ascended
Into a mist. And this
Is where we swim the brambles
And catch the path across
The late or early moor
Between us and the Gulvas.

3

Hold on to me and step
Over the world's thorns.
We shall soon be on
The yellow and emerald moss
Of the Penwith moor.
Are you all right beside me?
What's your name and age
As though I did not know.
Are we getting older
At different speeds differently?

4

No, that's not it. The Gulvas
Cannot be seen from here.
Have we left it too late
Maybe the Gulvas is too
Far on a day like this
For us what are our ages
What are our foreign names
What are we doing here
Wet and scratched with the Gulvas
Moving away before us?

5

Let us go back. Reader,
You who have observed
Us at your price from word
To word through the rain,
Dont be put down. I'll come
Again and take you on
The great walk to the Gulvas.
Be well wrapped up against
The high moor and the brambles.

AN ENTERTAINMENT FOR W. S. GRAHAM
FOR HIM HAVING REACHED SIXTY-FIVE

What are you going to do
With what is left of yourself
Now among the rustling
Of your maybe best years?
This is not an auto-elegy
With me pouring my heart
Out into where you
Differently stand or sit
On the Epidaurus steps.
What shall I say to myself
Having put myself down
On to a public page?

Where am I going now?
And where are you going
Tricked into reading
Words of my later life?
Let me pretend you are
Roughly of my age.
Are you a boy or a girl?
And what has happened to you?

Look at the chirping various
Leaves of Mr Graham's
Spanking summer. Where are
You at? I know my face
Has changed. My hair has blanched
Into a wrong disguise
Sitting on top of my head.

Beside each other perched
On the Epidaurus steps.
Where am I going to go?
Shall I rise to follow
The thin sound of the goats
Tinkling their bells?